30
MINUTES
OR LESS

Spicy
Food

30
MINUTES
OR LESS

Spicy
Food

p

This is a Parragon Book

First published in 2006

Parragon

Queen Street House

4 Queen Street

Bath BA1 1HE, UK

ISBN: 1-40547-384-3

Printed in China

Produced by the Bridgewater Book Company Ltd

Front cover photography by Mike Cooper

Front cover home economy by Sumi Glass

Notes for the Reader

This book uses metric and imperial measurements. Follow the same units of measurement throughout; do not mix metric and imperial. All spoon measurements are level: teaspoons are assumed to be 5 ml, and tablespoons are assumed to be 15 ml. Unless otherwise stated, milk is assumed to be full fat, eggs and individual vegetables are medium and pepper is freshly ground black pepper.

Recipes using raw or very lightly cooked eggs should be avoided by children, the elderly, pregnant women, convalescents and anyone suffering from an illness. Pregnant women and breast-feeding women are advised to avoid eating peanuts and peanut products.

Contents

Introduction

Sometimes even the most creative cook needs to spice up the menu, and there's nothing like a fiery flavour to brighten up the blandest of foods. This fabulous and inspiring selection of flavoursome and exotic dishes is a source of inspiration for anyone who enjoys eating spicy foods.

Written for anyone who enjoys eating spicy food but doesn't want to spend hours in the kitchen, these easy recipes have been specially chosen so that even the busiest person can enjoy delicious, fresh, home-cooked food, and quickly, too. All the recipes in this book can be completed in 30 minutes or under, or about the time it takes to heat through a supermarket ready meal. The recipes are all designed to be executed with the minimum of time and effort – there are no complicated cooking methods or elaborate presentations, nor will you need to use every pot and pan in the kitchen. Simple step-by-step instructions and full-colour photographs enable even the most inexperienced to cook with confidence and success.

The book is divided into four chapters: snacks and starters, fish, meat and vegetarian. Recipes have been inspired by regional cuisines from around the world, drawing on an astonishing range of tastes, and are guaranteed to satisfy even the most ardent fan of fiery foods or those who prefer rather more subtle, tangy aromas.

Most cultures have their own way of making foods sizzle with flavour and excitement. Even the most calorie-restrictive diet can be enhanced with spicy foods. And hot foods often mean healthy foods – there are numerous health benefits associated with eating garlic or chillies, for example, from reduced blood pressure to lower cholesterol levels. As an added bonus, spicy cooking masks the flavour of some nutrient-rich foods such as spinach or soya that many people find unpalatable, so you can reap their health benefits without having to endure their tastes.

SPICY STORECUPBOARD STAPLES

Don't rely on an ancient bottle of Tabasco sauce to tickle your taste buds – stock up on these key ingredients and you'll be able to whip up a sizzling, steamy and irresistible meal at the drop of a hat. There is an incredible variety of chillies, herbs and spices that you can use to create luscious flavours – just add, subtract or even substitute to suit your personal preferences.

DRIED CHILLIES, HERBS AND SPICES

In an ideal world, all herbs and spices would be fresh, but in reality this isn't always possible. Buy dried herbs and spices in small quantities because they become stale quite quickly, and keep out of sunlight. Here are a few suggestions for herbs and spices to keep in stock:

Black peppercorns

Cardamom (green pods)

Cayenne pepper

Chinese five-spice powder

Chillies (whole and/or crushed) and chilli powder

Cinnamon (whole and ground)

Cloves (whole and ground)

Coriander (fresh and ground)

Cumin (whole and ground)

Garam masala (Indian spice mix)

Kaffir lime leaves

Mace (ground)

Nutmeg (whole)

Paprika

Turmeric

Keep a supply of fresh root ginger, galangal (if you can find it), bird's eye chillies (and any other varieties you like), lemon grass stalks and fresh coriander in the freezer. To make the most of mustard, you'll need seeds, powder and paste. Bottled ingredients with a kick should include pimientos (peppers), Thai green curry paste, Thai red curry paste and Tabasco sauce.

If you want to create authentic and exciting recipes, you'll also need to stock up on Thai fish sauce, soy sauce, coconut milk, sesame oil and ghee, and maintain a constant supply of lemons, limes, garlic and shallots or onions. And make sure you've got a good range of grains and pasta in your storecupboard to offset those fiery flavours.

Turn up the heat on your everyday cooking with these easy to make, fun to eat, spicy favourites from around the world. Whether it's Mexican Eggs, Goan-style Seafood Curry or some Hot Chilli Pasta, you'll discover radiant flavours and enticing tastes.

Chapter One
Snacks and Starters

Spicy Crab Soup
25 minutes to the table

SERVES 4

ingredients

1 litre/1¾ pints chicken stock

2 tomatoes, peeled (see cook's tip),
   deseeded and finely chopped

2.5-cm/1-inch piece fresh root ginger,
   finely chopped

1 small fresh red chilli, deseeded and
   finely chopped

2 tbsp Chinese rice wine

1 tbsp rice vinegar

¾ tsp sugar

1 tbsp cornflour

2 tbsp water

175 g/6 oz white crabmeat, thawed
   if frozen or drained if canned

salt and pepper

2 spring onions, shredded, to garnish

method

Pour the stock into a large, heavy-based saucepan and add the tomatoes, ginger, chilli, rice wine, vinegar and sugar. Bring to the boil, then reduce the heat, cover and simmer for 10 minutes.

Blend the cornflour and water together in a jug, then stir into the soup. Simmer, stirring constantly, for 2 minutes, or until the soup thickens slightly.

Gently stir in the crabmeat and heat through for 2 minutes. Season to taste with salt and pepper, then ladle into warmed soup bowls and serve immediately, garnished with the shredded spring onions.

cook's tip

To peel tomatoes, cut a small cross in the base of each tomato with a sharp knife. Put in a heatproof bowl, cover with boiling water and leave for a minute or so. Remove with a slotted spoon and plunge into cold water. Drain and peel off the skins.

variation

Chinese rice wine and rice vinegar are available from some large supermarkets as well as from Chinese food shops. If Chinese rice wine is not available, then use the same amount of dry sherry instead and replace the rice vinegar with white wine vinegar.

Omelette Rolls
20 minutes to the table

MAKES 8

ingredients

4 large eggs

2 tbsp water

1 tbsp Thai soy sauce

6 spring onions, finely chopped

1 fresh red chilli, deseeded and
    finely chopped

1 tbsp vegetable or groundnut oil

1 tbsp Thai green curry paste

bunch of fresh coriander, chopped,
    2 sprigs reserved to garnish

method

Beat the eggs, water and soy sauce together in a bowl. Set aside.
Put the spring onions and chilli in a mortar and pound with a pestle to
a paste.

   Heat half the oil in a 20-cm/8-inch frying pan over a medium heat.
Pour in half the egg mixture. Tilt to coat the base of the frying pan
evenly and cook until set. Lift out and set aside. Heat the remaining oil
in the frying pan and make a second omelette in the same way.

   Spread half the spring onion and chilli paste and curry paste in a thin
layer over each omelette and sprinkle the chopped coriander on top.
Roll up tightly. Cut each roll in half and then cut each piece diagonally
in half again. Serve immediately, while still warm, garnished with the
coriander sprigs.

Crispy Spring Rolls
30 minutes to the table

method

Heat the oil in a preheated wok or large frying pan over a high heat. Add the spring onions and chilli and stir-fry for 30 seconds. Add the carrot, courgette and red pepper and stir-fry for 1 minute. Remove from heat and stir in the beansprouts, bamboo shoots, soy sauce and chilli sauce. Taste and add more soy sauce or chilli sauce, if necessary.

Lay a spring roll wrapper on a work surface and spoon some of the vegetable mixture diagonally across the centre. Roll one corner over the filling and flip the sides of the wrapper over the top, to enclose the filling. Continue to roll up to make an enclosed parcel. Repeat with the remaining wrappers and filling to make 8 spring rolls.

Heat the oil for deep-frying in a preheated wok or large frying pan to 180–190°C/350–375°F, or until a cube of bread browns in 30 seconds. Add the spring rolls, in 2 batches, and cook until crisp and golden brown. Remove with a slotted spoon, drain on kitchen paper and keep hot while you cook the remaining spring rolls, then serve immediately.

MAKES 8

ingredients

2 tbsp vegetable or groundnut oil, plus extra for deep-frying
6 spring onions, cut into 5-cm/2-inch lengths
1 fresh green chilli, deseeded and chopped
1 carrot, cut into thin batons
1 courgette, cut into thin batons
½ red pepper, deseeded and thinly sliced
115 g/4 oz beansprouts, drained and rinsed if canned
115 g/4 oz canned bamboo shoots, drained and rinsed
3 tbsp Thai soy sauce
1–2 tbsp chilli sauce
8 spring roll wrappers

Spicy Beef and Noodle Soup

20 minutes to the table

SERVES 4

ingredients

1 litre/1¾ pints beef stock

150 ml/5 fl oz vegetable or
  groundnut oil

85 g/3 oz dried rice vermicelli
  noodles

2 shallots, thinly sliced

2 garlic cloves, crushed

2.5-cm/1-inch piece fresh root ginger,
  thinly sliced

225 g/8 oz fillet steak, cut into
  thin strips

2 tbsp Thai green curry paste

2 tbsp Thai soy sauce

1 tbsp Thai fish sauce

chopped fresh coriander, to garnish

method

Pour the stock into a large saucepan and bring to the boil. Meanwhile, heat the oil in a preheated wok or large frying pan. Add about one-third of the noodles and cook, stirring, for 10-20 seconds until puffed up. Lift out with tongs, drain on kitchen paper and set aside. Pour off all but 2 tablespoons of the oil from the wok.

Add the shallots, garlic and ginger to the wok and stir-fry for 1 minute. Add the beef and curry paste and stir-fry for 3-4 minutes until tender.

Transfer the beef mixture to the saucepan of stock with the uncooked noodles, soy sauce and fish sauce. Simmer for 2-3 minutes until the noodles have swelled. Serve hot, garnished with chopped coriander and the reserved crispy noodles.

Scallops on Noodles
20 minutes to the table

method

Cook the noodles in a large saucepan of boiling water for 1½ minutes, or according to the packet instructions, until tender, then rinse under cold running water and drain well. Meanwhile, melt the butter in a small saucepan over a low heat. Add the garlic and cook, stirring, for 1 minute. Stir in the paprika and set aside.

Heat the oil in a preheated wok or large frying pan over a high heat. Stir in the curry paste, water and soy sauce and bring to the boil. Add the cooked noodles and reheat, stirring gently. Stir in the spring onions, then remove from the heat and keep warm.

Heat a ridged, cast-iron grill pan over a high heat and brush lightly with oil. Add the scallops to the pan and cook, brushing with the garlic butter, for 3 minutes, then turn over and cook for no more than 2 minutes on the other side until just cooked (the centre shouldn't be totally opaque if cut open). Season to taste with salt and pepper. Divide the noodles between 4 individual dishes and top with 3 scallops each. Garnish with spring onion slices.

cook's tip

This is an excellent dish to serve at a dinner party, but you have to be organized. You can boil the noodles and make the garlic butter for cooking the scallops ahead of time, but, as everything else is done at the last minute, it's a good idea to have your guests seated when you start cooking. You want the scallops to go from the pan to the table as quickly as possible.

SERVES 4

ingredients

115 g/4 oz dried green tea noodles, or the thinnest green noodles you can find

25 g/1 oz butter

1 garlic clove, crushed

pinch of paprika

1 tbsp groundnut or sunflower oil, plus extra for brushing

2 tbsp Thai green curry paste

2 tbsp water

2 tsp light soy sauce

2 spring onions, finely shredded, plus extra, sliced, to garnish

12 fresh raw scallops, shucked

salt and pepper

Indonesian Sweetcorn Balls

20 minutes to the table

SERVES 4

ingredients

115 g/4 oz unsalted peanuts
325 g/11½ oz canned sweetcorn
   kernels, drained
1 onion, finely chopped
115 g/4 oz plain flour
1 tsp ground coriander
½ tsp sambal ulek or chilli sauce
1-2 tbsp warm water (optional)
groundnut oil, for deep-frying
salt

method

Put the peanuts in a food processor and process briefly until coarsely ground. Alternatively, grind them in a mortar with a pestle. Transfer to a bowl and stir in the sweetcorn kernels, onion, flour, coriander and sambal ulek. Season to taste with salt. Knead to a dough, adding the warm water, if necessary, to make the dough workable.

Heat the oil in a deep-fryer or large, heavy-based saucepan to 180-190°C/350-375°F, or until a cube of bread browns in 30 seconds. Using your hands, form tablespoonfuls of the dough into balls. Add the sweetcorn balls to the pan, in batches, and cook until golden and crisp.

Remove with a slotted spoon, drain on kitchen paper and keep hot while you cook the remaining sweetcorn balls. Serve immediately or leave to cool before serving.

cook's tip

Sambal ulek is a fiery hot chilli sauce available from Asian food shops and supermarkets. If you cannot find it, use chilli sauce instead.

Whitebait with Green Chilli sauce

20 minutes to the table

method

Cook the fish in a large saucepan of boiling water for 30 seconds-
2 minutes until the flesh is turning soft but not breaking up. Drain and
leave to cool.

Meanwhile, to make the sauce, heat the oil in a small saucepan over
a high heat until smoking. Add the chilli and cook, turning frequently,
until the skin blisters. Remove and leave to cool. When cool enough to
handle, peel off the skin and finely chop the flesh. Leave to cool, then
mix with all the other sauce ingredients in a bowl.

To serve, pour the sauce over the fish and serve immediately.

cook's tip

The fish have a tendency to stick together and break easily once
cooked, so treat with care.

SERVES 4

ingredients

175 g/6 oz whitebait

SAUCE
1 tbsp vegetable or groundnut oil
1 large fresh green chilli
2 drops of sesame oil
1 tbsp light soy sauce
pinch of salt
pinch of sugar
1 garlic clove, finely chopped

Mexican Eggs
20 minutes to the table

SERVES 4

ingredients

8 large eggs

2 tbsp milk

1 tsp olive oil

1 red pepper, deseeded and thinly
sliced

½ fresh red chilli, finely chopped

1 fresh chorizo sausage, outer casing
removed, sliced

4 tbsp chopped fresh coriander

pepper

4 slices toasted wholemeal bread,
to serve

method

Beat the eggs, milk and pepper to taste together in a large bowl, then
set aside.

Heat the oil in a non-stick frying pan over a medium heat. Add the
red pepper and chilli and cook, stirring frequently, for 5 minutes, or
until the red pepper is softened and browned in places. Add the chorizo
and cook, stirring frequently, until just browned. Transfer to a warmed
plate and set aside.

Return the frying pan to the heat, add the egg mixture and cook,
stirring with a wooden spoon, to a soft scramble. Add the chorizo
mixture, stir to combine and scatter over the coriander.

Serve immediately on toasted wholemeal bread.

Chorizo Empanadillas
30 minutes to the table

MAKES 12

ingredients

250 g/9 oz ready-made puff pastry,
   thawed if frozen
plain flour, for dusting
125 g/4½ oz cured chorizo sausage,
   outer casing removed, cut into
   1-cm/½-inch dice
beaten egg, to glaze
paprika, to garnish

method

Preheat the oven to 200ºC/400ºF/Gas Mark 6. Sprinkle 2 baking sheets with water.

Roll out the pastry thinly on a lightly floured work surface. Using a plain, round 8-cm/3¼-inch cutter, cut out 12 rounds. Put about a teaspoon of the diced chorizo onto one half of each pastry round.

Dampen the edge of each pastry round with a little water, then fold the plain half over the chorizo to cover. Seal the edges together with your fingers. Using the prongs of a fork, press against the edges to give a decorative finish and seal them further. With the tip of a sharp knife, make a small slit in the side of each pastry. You can store the pastries, covered, in the refrigerator at this stage until you are ready to bake.

Transfer the pastries to the prepared baking sheets and brush each with a little beaten egg to glaze. Bake in the preheated oven for 10-15 minutes until golden brown and well risen. Using a small sieve, lightly dust the top of each empanadilla with paprika to garnish. Serve the empanadillas hot or warm.

cook's tip

Serve as a delicious tapa with a glass of chilled white wine.

Laksa
30 minutes to the table

method

Heat the oil in a large saucepan over a medium heat. Add the garlic, chillies, lemon grass and ginger and cook, stirring frequently, for 5 minutes. Add the stock and bring to the boil, then reduce the heat and simmer for 5 minutes.

Stir in the prawns, mushrooms and carrot. If using the egg noodles, break into small lengths, add to the saucepan and simmer for a further 5 minutes, or until the prawns have turned pink and the noodles are just tender.

Stir in the fish sauce and coriander and heat through for a further minute before serving.

variation

Use a pack of mixed oriental mushrooms in place of the shiitake mushrooms, if available.

SERVES 4

ingredients

1 tbsp sunflower oil

2–3 garlic cloves, cut into thin slivers

1–2 fresh red bird's eye chillies, deseeded and sliced

2 lemon grass stalks, outer leaves removed, chopped

2.5-cm/1-inch piece fresh root ginger, grated

1.2 litres/2 pints fish or vegetable stock

350 g/12 oz large raw prawns, peeled and deveined

115 g/4 oz shiitake mushrooms, sliced

1 large carrot, grated

55 g/2 oz dried egg noodles (optional)

1–2 tsp Thai fish sauce

1 tbsp chopped fresh coriander

Chapter Two
Fish and Seafood

Chillies Stuffed with Fish Paste

30 minutes to the table

method

Mix all the ingredients for the marinade together in a bowl. Add the fish and toss to coat in the marinade. Cover and leave to marinate in a cool place while you prepare the chillies and beans.

Cut the chillies in half lengthways and scoop out the seeds and white veins. Cut into bite-sized pieces.

Add the egg to the fish mixture and mix to a smooth paste. Spread each piece of chilli with about ½ teaspoon of the fish paste. Heat the oil in a preheated wok or deep saucepan over a high heat. Add the chilli pieces and cook on both sides until beginning to brown. Remove with a slotted spoon and drain on kitchen paper.

Pour off all but 1 tablespoon of the oil from the wok and heat over a high heat. Add the garlic and stir-fry for 1 minute, or until fragrant. Stir in the beans and mix well. Stir in the soy sauce and sugar, then add the chilli pieces. Add the water, cover and simmer over a low heat for 5 minutes. Serve immediately.

variation

This dish can also be made with bitter melon (sometimes known as bitter gourd), which should be prepared in the same way as the chillies, but blanched before being topped with the fish paste.

SERVES 4-6

ingredients

225 g/8 oz white fish, minced
4-6 fresh mild red and green chillies
½ tbsp fermented black beans, rinsed
    and lightly mashed
2 tbsp lightly beaten egg
vegetable or groundnut oil, for
    shallow-frying
2 garlic cloves, finely chopped
1 tbsp light soy sauce
pinch of sugar
1 tbsp water

MARINADE

1 tsp finely chopped fresh root ginger
pinch of salt
pinch of white pepper
½ tsp vegetable or groundnut oil

Fish Curry with Rice Noodles

25 minutes to the table

SERVES 4-6

ingredients

2 tbsp vegetable or groundnut oil

1 large onion, chopped

2 garlic cloves, chopped

85 g/3 oz button mushrooms

225 g/8 oz skinless monkfish fillet,
   cut into 2.5-cm/1-inch cubes

225 g/8 oz skinless salmon fillet,
   cut into 2.5-cm/1-inch cubes

225 g/8 oz skinless cod fillet,
   cut into 2.5-cm/1-inch cubes

2 tbsp Thai red curry paste

400 ml/14 fl oz canned coconut milk

handful of fresh coriander, chopped

1 tsp palm sugar or soft light
   brown sugar

1 tsp Thai fish sauce

115 g/4 oz dried rice noodles

3 spring onions, chopped

55 g/2 oz fresh beansprouts

handful of fresh Thai basil sprigs

method

Heat the oil in a preheated wok or large frying pan over a medium heat. Add the onion, garlic and mushrooms and cook, stirring frequently, for 5 minutes, or until softened but not browned.

Add all the fish, curry paste and coconut milk and bring slowly to the boil. Reduce the heat and simmer for 2-3 minutes. Stir in half the coriander, the sugar and fish sauce. Set aside and keep warm.

Meanwhile, soak the noodles in a saucepan of just-boiled water for 3-4 minutes, or according to the packet instructions, until tender, then drain well using a colander. Set the colander and noodles over a saucepan of simmering water. Add the spring onions, beansprouts and most of the basil and steam on top of the noodles for 1-2 minutes, or until just wilted.

Pile the noodles onto warmed serving plates and top with the fish curry. Scatter the remaining coriander over the top, garnish with the remaining basil sprigs and serve immediately.

cook's tip

Coconut milk is used frequently in Thai curries, to flavour and enrich them. It is not, however, as one might think, the liquid inside a coconut. Coconut milk is actually made from the flesh of fresh coconut, which is grated and pressed and then combined with water.

Wok-fried King Prawns in Spicy Sauce

20 minutes to the table

SERVES 4

ingredients

3 tbsp vegetable or groundnut oil

450 g/1 lb raw king prawns, deveined
   but unpeeled

2 tsp finely chopped fresh root ginger

1 tsp finely chopped garlic

1 tbsp chopped spring onion

2 tbsp chilli bean sauce

1 tsp Chinese rice wine

1 tsp sugar

½ tsp light soy sauce

1-2 tbsp chicken stock

method

Heat the oil in a preheated wok or deep saucepan over a high heat. Add the prawns and stir-fry for 4 minutes. Push the prawns up the side of the wok out of the oil, then add the ginger and garlic and stir-fry for 1 minute, or until fragrant. Add the spring onion and chilli bean sauce, and stir in the prawns.

Reduce the heat slightly and add the rice wine, sugar, soy sauce and stock. Cover and cook for a further minute. Serve immediately.

cook's tip

Increase the amount of chilli bean sauce to create a hotter dish, if you prefer.

Tagliatelle with Hake in Chilli Sauce

25 minutes to the table

method

Using a sharp knife, chop the parsley, garlic and chilli together. Heat half the oil in a large, heavy-based frying pan over a low heat. Add the herb mixture and cook, stirring, for 1-2 minutes, or until the garlic is fragrant. Add the fish, re-cover and cook for 5 minutes, then turn the fish and cook for a further 5 minutes. Add the tomatoes and season to taste with salt and pepper, then re-cover and simmer for a further 5 minutes.

Meanwhile, bring a large, heavy-based saucepan of lightly salted water to the boil. Add the pasta, return to the boil, and cook for 8-10 minutes, or according to the packet instructions, until tender but still firm to the bite.

Drain the pasta and return to the saucepan. Drizzle with the remaining oil and toss to coat. Transfer to a warmed serving platter and top with the fish mixture. Serve immediately.

cook's tip

Make sure that you remove any fine bones remaining in the fish fillets. This is most easily done with tweezers.

SERVES 4

ingredients

bunch of fresh parsley

1 garlic clove

1 dried red chilli, deseeded

5 tbsp olive oil

450 g/1 lb hake fillets, skinned and cut into chunks

350 g/12 oz tomatoes, peeled, deseeded and diced

350 g/12 oz dried tagliatelle

salt and pepper

Prawn and Pineapple Curry

20 minutes to the table

SERVES 4

ingredients

450 ml/16 fl oz coconut cream

½ fresh pineapple, peeled, cored
  and chopped

2 tbsp Thai red curry paste

2 tbsp Thai fish sauce

2 tsp sugar

350 g/12 oz raw tiger prawns, peeled
  and deveined

2 tbsp chopped fresh coriander, plus
  extra to garnish

jasmine rice, to serve

method

Heat the coconut cream, pineapple, curry paste, fish sauce and sugar in a saucepan over a medium heat until almost boiling. Stir in the prawns and coriander, reduce the heat and simmer gently for 3 minutes, or until the prawns have turned pink.

Sprinkle with extra coriander and serve immediately with cooked jasmine rice.

Scallops in Black Bean Sauce

15 minutes to the table

SERVES 4

ingredients

2 tbsp vegetable or groundnut oil

1 tsp finely chopped garlic

1 tsp finely chopped fresh root ginger

1 tbsp fermented black beans, rinsed
  and lightly mashed

400 g/14 oz fresh raw scallops,
  shucked

½ tsp light soy sauce

1 tsp Chinese rice wine

1 tsp sugar

3–4 fresh red bird's-eye chillies,
  finely chopped

1–2 tsp chicken stock

1 tbsp finely chopped spring onion

method

Heat the oil in a preheated wok or deep saucepan over a high heat. Add the garlic and stir, then add the ginger and stir-fry together for 1 minute, or until fragrant. Mix in the beans, toss in the scallops and stir-fry for 1 minute. Add the soy sauce, rice wine, sugar and chillies.

Reduce the heat and simmer for 2 minutes, adding the stock, if necessary. Add the spring onion, stir and serve immediately.

cook's tip

Fresh scallops, removed from their shells, are always preferable, but frozen scallops also work well in this strongly flavoured dish.

Mussels with Mustard Seeds and Shallots

30 minutes to the table

method

Firstly, discard any mussels with broken shells, or any that refuse to close when tapped.

Heat the oil in a preheated kadhai, wok or large frying pan over a medium-high heat. Add the mustard seeds and cook, stirring, for 1 minute, or until beginning to jump.

Add the shallots and garlic and cook, stirring frequently, for 3 minutes, or until beginning to brown. Stir in the vinegar, chillies, dissolved creamed coconut, curry leaves, turmeric, chilli powder and a pinch of salt and bring to the boil, stirring.

Reduce the heat to very low. Add the mussels, cover the kadhai and simmer, shaking the pan frequently, for 3-4 minutes, or until the mussels are opened. Discard any that remain closed. Ladle the mussels into deep bowls, then taste the sauce and add extra salt, if necessary. Spoon over the mussels and serve immediately.

cook's tip

Peeling a large number of shallots like this can be time-consuming, but the job is quicker if you submerge them beforehand in a saucepan of boiling water for 30-45 seconds. Drain the shallots and use a knife to slice off the root end, then they should peel easily.

SERVES 4

ingredients

2 kg/4 lb 8 oz live mussels, scrubbed and debearded

3 tbsp vegetable or groundnut oil

½ tbsp black mustard seeds

8 shallots, chopped

2 garlic cloves, crushed

2 tbsp distilled vinegar

4 small fresh red chillies

85 g/3 oz creamed coconut, grated and dissolved in 300 ml/10 fl oz boiling water

10 fresh curry leaves or 1 tbsp dried

½ tsp ground turmeric

¼-½ tsp chilli powder

salt

Goan-style Seafood Curry

30 minutes to the table

SERVES 4-6

ingredients

3 tbsp vegetable or groundnut oil

1 tbsp black mustard seeds

12 fresh curry leaves or 1 tbsp dried

6 shallots, finely chopped

1 garlic clove, crushed

1 tsp ground turmeric

½ tsp ground coriander

¼–½ tsp chilli powder

140 g/5 oz creamed coconut, grated and dissolved in 300 ml/10 fl oz boiling water

500 g/1 lb 2 oz skinless white fish fillets, such as monkfish or cod, cut into large chunks

450 g/1 lb large raw prawns, peeled and deveined

juice and finely grated rind of 1 lime

salt

lime wedges, to serve

method

Heat the oil in a preheated kadhai, wok or large frying pan over a high heat. Add the mustard seeds and cook, stirring, for 1 minute, or until they begin to jump. Stir in the curry leaves.

Add the shallots and garlic and cook, stirring frequently, for 5 minutes, or until the shallots are golden. Stir in the turmeric, coriander and chilli powder and cook, stirring, for 30 seconds.

Add the dissolved creamed coconut. Bring to the boil, then reduce the heat to medium and cook, stirring, for 2 minutes.

Reduce the heat to low, add the fish and simmer for 1 minute, spooning the sauce over the fish and very gently stirring it around. Add the prawns and simmer for a further 4–5 minutes until the fish flesh flakes easily and the prawns have turned pink.

Add half the lime juice, then taste and add more lime juice and salt to taste. Sprinkle with the lime rind and serve with lime wedges.

Crab and Coriander Salad

15 minutes to the table

method

Put the crabmeat in a bowl and stir in the spring onions and coriander.

Mix all the ingredients for the dressing together in a jug. Arrange the shredded lettuce on a serving platter and scatter with the cucumber.

Arrange the crab salad over the lettuce and drizzle the dressing over the salad. Serve immediately.

SERVES 4

ingredients

350 g/12 oz canned
white crabmeat, drained
4 spring onions, finely chopped
handful of fresh coriander, chopped,
plus extra sprigs to garnish
1 Webbs lettuce, shredded
7.5-cm/3-inch piece cucumber,
chopped

DRESSING
1 garlic clove, crushed
2.5-cm/1-inch piece root ginger,
grated
2 lime leaves, torn into pieces
juice of 1 lime
1 tsp Thai fish sauce

Malaysian-style Coconut Noodles with Prawns

25 minutes to the table

SERVES 4

ingredients

2 tbsp vegetable oil

1 small red pepper, deseeded
    and diced

200 g/7 oz pak choi, stalks thinly
    sliced and leaves chopped

2 large garlic cloves, chopped

1 tsp ground turmeric

2 tsp garam masala

1 tsp chilli powder (optional)

125 ml/4 fl oz hot vegetable stock

2 heaped tbsp smooth peanut butter

350 ml/12 fl oz coconut milk

1 tbsp tamari (wheat-free soy sauce)

250 g/9 oz dried rice noodles

280 g/10 oz large cooked
    peeled prawns

TO GARNISH

2 spring onions, finely shredded

1 tbsp sesame seeds

method

Heat the oil in a preheated wok or large, heavy-based frying pan over a high heat. Add the red pepper, pak choi stalks and garlic and stir-fry for 3 minutes. Add the turmeric, garam masala, chilli powder, if using, and pak choi leaves and stir-fry for a further minute.

Mix the hot stock and peanut butter together in a heatproof bowl until the peanut butter has dissolved, then add to the stir-fry with the coconut milk and tamari. Cook over a medium heat for 5 minutes, or until reduced and thickened.

Meanwhile, soak the noodles in a saucepan of just-boiled water for 3-4 minutes, or according to the packet instructions, until tender, then drain and refresh the noodles under cold running water. Add the noodles and prawns to the curry and cook, stirring frequently, for a further 2-3 minutes until heated through.

Serve the noodle dish immediately, sprinkled with the shredded spring onions and sesame seeds.

Chapter Three
Meat

Pepperoni Pasta
25 minutes to the table

SERVES 4

ingredients

3 tbsp olive oil

1 onion, chopped

1 red pepper, deseeded and diced

1 orange pepper, deseeded and diced

800 g/1 lb 12 oz canned
   chopped tomatoes in juice

1 tbsp sun-dried tomato paste

1 tsp paprika

225 g/8 oz pepperoni sausage, sliced

2 tbsp chopped fresh flat-leaf parsley,
   plus extra to garnish

450 g/1 lb dried garganelli

salt and pepper

mixed salad leaves, to serve

method

Heat 2 tablespoons of the oil in a large, heavy-based frying pan over a medium heat. Add the onion and cook, stirring occasionally, for 5 minutes, or until softened. Stir in the red and orange peppers, tomatoes with their juice, sun-dried tomato paste and paprika and bring to the boil.

Add the pepperoni and parsley and season to taste with salt and pepper. Stir well and bring to the boil, then reduce the heat and simmer for 10-15 minutes.

Meanwhile, bring a large, heavy-based saucepan of lightly salted water to the boil. Add the pasta, return to the boil and cook for 8-10 minutes, or according to the packet instructions, until tender but still firm to the bite. Drain well and transfer to a warmed serving dish. Add the remaining oil and toss to coat. Add the sauce and toss again. Sprinkle with parsley to garnish and serve immediately with mixed salad leaves.

variation

If you cannot find garganelli pasta, then use penne or another pasta shape, such as fusilli bucati or farfalle.

cook's tip

Pepperoni is a hotly spiced Italian sausage made from pork and beef, and is flavoured with fennel. You could substitute other spicy sausages, such as kabanos or chorizo, if you like.

Spicy Beef
30 minutes to the table

SERVES 4

ingredients

225 g/8 oz fillet steak
2 garlic cloves, crushed
1 tsp ground star anise
1 tbsp dark soy sauce

SAUCE
2 tbsp vegetable oil
bunch of spring onions,
    halved lengthways
1 tbsp dark soy sauce
1 tbsp dry sherry
¼ tsp chilli sauce
150 ml/5 fl oz water
2 tsp cornflour
4 tsp water

method

Cut the steak into thin strips and put in a shallow dish.

Mix the garlic, star anise and soy sauce together in a small bowl and pour over the steak strips, turning to coat in the marinade. Cover and leave to marinate at room temperature for 15 minutes.

Heat the oil in a preheated wok or large frying pan over a high heat. Reduce the heat, add the halved spring onions and stir-fry for 1–2 minutes. Remove from the wok with a slotted spoon and set aside.

Add the beef to the wok, together with the marinade, and stir-fry for 3–4 minutes. Return the halved spring onions to the wok and add the soy sauce, sherry, chilli sauce and two-thirds of the water.

Blend the cornflour with the remaining water in a jug and stir into the wok. Bring to the boil and cook, stirring constantly, until the sauce thickens and clears.

Transfer to a warmed serving dish and serve immediately.

Stir-fried Lamb
25 minutes to the table

method

Heat the oil in a preheated wok or large, heavy-based frying pan over a high heat. Add the lamb and stir-fry for 2–3 minutes, or until browned all over. Remove with a slotted spoon and drain on kitchen paper.

Add the onion, garlic and chillies to the wok and stir-fry for 3 minutes. Add the mangetout and stir-fry for 2 minutes, then stir in the spinach leaves and return the lamb to the wok.

Add the lime juice, oyster sauce, fish sauce and sugar and cook, stirring constantly, for 4 minutes, or until the lamb is cooked through and tender. Stir in the mint, season to taste with salt and pepper and serve immediately.

variations

Replace the lime juice with the same amount of lemon juice, and if you don't like it too hot, use just 1 fresh red chilli.

cook's tip

Oyster sauce is a thick soy sauce, which is flavoured with oyster juice. The taste is very delicate and is ideal for dishes that need livening up. It is found in most supermarkets and Chinese food shops.

SERVES 4

ingredients

4 tbsp groundnut oil
550 g/1 lb 4 oz neck fillet of lamb, thinly sliced
1 large onion, finely chopped
2 garlic cloves, finely chopped
2 fresh red chillies, deseeded and thinly sliced
175 g/6 oz mangetout
350 g/12 oz fresh spinach leaves
2 tbsp lime juice
3 tbsp oyster sauce
2 tbsp Thai fish sauce
2 tsp caster sugar
5 tbsp chopped fresh mint
salt and pepper

Griddled Steak with Hot Chilli Salsa

20 minutes to the table

SERVES 4

ingredients

4 sirloin steaks, about 225 g/8 oz
    each
sunflower oil, for brushing
salt and pepper

HOT CHILLI SALSA
4 fresh red habanero or Scotch
    bonnet chillies
4 fresh green poblano chillies
3 tomatoes, peeled, deseeded
    and diced
2 tbsp chopped fresh coriander
1 tbsp red wine vinegar
2 tbsp olive oil
salt

method

To make the salsa, preheat the grill to high. Arrange the chillies on a baking sheet and cook under the preheated grill, turning frequently, until blackened and charred. Leave to cool. When cool enough to handle, peel off the skins. Halve and deseed the chillies, then finely chop the flesh.

Mix the chillies, tomatoes and coriander together in a bowl. Whisk the vinegar and oil together in a jug, season to taste with salt and pour over the salsa. Toss well, cover and chill in the refrigerator until required.

Heat a ridged, cast-iron grill pan over a medium heat and brush lightly with oil. Season the steaks to taste with salt and pepper, add to the griddle pan and cook for 2–4 minutes on each side, or until cooked to your liking. Serve immediately with the salsa.

Pad Thai
25 minutes to the table

method

Soak the noodles in a saucepan of just-boiled water for 10 minutes, or until only just tender, then drain well and set aside.

Meanwhile, heat the oil in a wok or large frying pan over a high heat. Add the garlic, chillies and pork and stir-fry for 2-3 minutes. Add the prawns and stir-fry for 2-3 minutes.

Add the chives and noodles, then cover and heat through for 1-2 minutes. Add the fish sauce, lime juice, sugar and eggs and cook, stirring and tossing constantly to mix in the eggs, for 2 minutes.

Stir in the beansprouts, coriander and peanuts. Garnish with coriander sprigs and serve immediately with extra chopped peanuts and small dishes of crispy fried onions.

SERVES 4

ingredients

225 g/8 oz dried thick rice stick
    noodles
2 tbsp vegetable or groundnut oil
2 garlic cloves, chopped
2 fresh red chillies, deseeded and
    chopped
175 g/6 oz pork fillet, thinly sliced
115 g/4 oz raw prawns,
    peeled, deveined and chopped
8 fresh Chinese chives, snipped
2 tbsp Thai fish sauce
juice of 1 lime
2 tsp palm sugar or soft
    light brown sugar
2 eggs, beaten
115 g/4 oz fresh beansprouts
4 tbsp chopped fresh coriander,
    plus extra sprigs to garnish
115 g/4 oz unsalted peanuts,
    chopped, plus extra to serve
crispy fried onions, to serve

Pork with Mixed Green Beans

20 minutes to the table

method

Heat the oil in a preheated wok or large frying pan over a high heat. Add the shallots, pork, galangal and garlic and stir-fry for 3-4 minutes until the pork is lightly browned all over.

Add the stock, chilli sauce and peanut butter and cook, stirring, until the peanut butter has melted. Add all the beans, stir well and simmer for 3-4 minutes, or until tender and the pork is cooked through. Serve immediately with crispy noodles.

SERVES 4

ingredients

2 tbsp vegetable or groundnut oil
2 shallots, chopped
225 g/8 oz pork fillet, thinly sliced
2.5-cm/1-inch piece fresh galangal or
    root ginger, thinly sliced
2 garlic cloves, chopped
300 ml/10 fl oz chicken stock
4 tbsp chilli sauce
4 tbsp crunchy peanut butter
115 g/4 oz fine French beans
115 g/4 oz frozen broad beans
115 g/4 oz runner beans, sliced
crispy noodles, to serve

Minced Chicken Skewers
20 minutes to the table

MAKES 8

ingredients

450 g/1 lb fresh chicken mince

1 onion, finely chopped

1 fresh red chilli, deseeded and
chopped

2 tbsp Thai red curry paste

1 tsp palm sugar or soft light brown
sugar

1 tsp ground coriander

1 tsp ground cumin

1 egg white

8 lemon grass stalks

rice with chopped spring onion, to
serve

method

Mix the chicken, onion, chilli, curry paste and sugar together in a
bowl to a thick paste. Stir in the coriander, cumin and egg white and
mix again.

Preheat the grill to high. Divide the mixture into 8 equal portions and
squeeze them around each of the lemon grass stalks. Arrange on a grill
rack and cook under the preheated grill, turning frequently, for
8 minutes, or until browned and cooked through. Serve immediately,
with cooked rice with chopped spring onion stirred through it.

Stir-fried Chicken with Thai Basil

25 minutes to the table

method

Heat the oil in a preheated wok or large frying pan over a high heat. Add the garlic and spring onions and stir-fry for 1-2 minutes, or until the spring onions are softened.

Add the chillies and green pepper and stir-fry for 2 minutes.

Add the chicken and stir-fry for 3-4 minutes until browned all over. Add the chopped basil and fish sauce and stir-fry for a further 3-4 minutes, or until the chicken is cooked through. Garnish with basil sprigs and serve immediately with cooked rice.

SERVES 4

ingredients

2 tbsp vegetable oil

4 garlic cloves, crushed

4 spring onions, finely chopped

4 fresh green chillies, deseeded and finely chopped

1 green pepper, deseeded and thinly sliced

600 g/1 lb 5 oz skinless, boneless chicken breasts, cut into thin strips

25 g/1 oz fresh Thai basil leaves, roughly chopped, plus extra sprigs to garnish

2 tbsp Thai fish sauce

rice, to serve

Chicken with Pak Choi
20 minutes to the table

SERVES 4

ingredients

175 g/6 oz broccoli

1 tbsp groundnut oil

2.5-cm/1-inch piece fresh root ginger, finely grated

1 fresh red bird's eye chilli, deseeded and chopped

2 garlic cloves, crushed

1 red onion, cut into wedges

450 g/1 lb skinless, boneless chicken breasts, cut into thin strips

175 g/6 oz pak choi, shredded

115 g/4 oz baby sweetcorn, halved

1 tbsp light soy sauce

1 tbsp Thai fish sauce

1 tbsp chopped fresh coriander

1 tbsp toasted sesame seeds

method

Break the broccoli into small florets and cook in a saucepan of lightly salted boiling water for 3 minutes, then drain.

Meanwhile, heat the oil in a preheated wok or large frying pan over a high heat. Add the ginger, chilli and garlic and stir-fry for 1 minute. Add the onion and chicken and stir-fry for 3-4 minutes, or until the chicken is browned all over.

Add the remaining vegetables, including the broccoli, and stir-fry for 3-4 minutes, or until tender and the chicken is cooked through.

Add the soy sauce and fish sauce and stir-fry for a further 1-2 minutes, then serve immediately, sprinkled with the coriander and sesame seeds.

Chicken Curry with Mushrooms and Beans

30 minutes to the table

SERVES 4-6

ingredients

55 g/2 oz ghee or 4 tbsp vegetable
   or groundnut oil
8 skinless, boneless chicken
   thighs, sliced
1 small onion, chopped
2 large garlic cloves, crushed
100 g/3½ oz green beans
100 g/3½ oz mushrooms,
   thickly sliced
2 tbsp milk
salt and pepper
fresh coriander sprigs, to garnish

CURRY PASTE
2 tsp garam masala
1 tsp mild, medium or hot curry
   powder, to taste
1 tbsp water

method

To make the curry paste, put the garam masala and curry powder in a bowl and stir in the water, then set aside.

Melt half the ghee in a large, heavy-based saucepan or frying pan with a tight-fitting lid over a medium-high heat. Add the chicken and curry paste and cook, stirring frequently, for 5 minutes.

Add the onion, garlic and beans and cook, stirring frequently, for a further 5 minutes, or until the chicken is cooked through.

Add the remaining ghee and mushrooms and, when the ghee melts, stir in the milk. Season to taste with salt and pepper. Reduce the heat to low, cover and simmer, stirring occasionally, for 10 minutes. Serve the curry immediately, garnished with fresh coriander.

Chapter Four
Vegetarian

Spiced Lentil Salad with Goat's Cheese

30 minutes to the table

SERVES 4

ingredients

1 tbsp olive oil, plus extra for brushing

2 red onions, finely sliced

2 garlic cloves, crushed

1 fresh red chilli, deseeded and finely chopped

½ tsp ground turmeric

½ tsp ground cumin

½ tsp ground coriander

1 cinnamon stick

2 star anise

5 green cardamom pods, gently crushed

1 small piece fresh root ginger, finely chopped

200 g/7 oz Puy lentils

700 ml/1¼ pints vegetable stock

4 firm goat's cheeses with rind (chèvre), 100 g/3½ oz each

70 g/2½ oz sunblush tomatoes, cut into strips

2 tbsp pine kernels, toasted

bunch of fresh coriander, leaves only

salt and pepper

method

Heat the oil in a non-stick frying pan over a medium-high heat. Add three-quarters of the onions, the garlic, chilli, spices and ginger and cook, stirring frequently, for 3–5 minutes, or until the onions are softened.

Add the lentils and stir to coat in the onion mixture, then add the stock and salt and pepper to taste. Bring to the boil, then reduce the heat and simmer, stirring occasionally, for 15–20 minutes until all the liquid is absorbed and the lentils are tender. Remove the cinnamon stick, star anise and cardamom pods. Leave the lentils to cool slightly so that they are warm rather than hot.

Meanwhile, preheat the grill to high. Line the grill pan with foil and brush with a little oil. Put the cheeses in the grill pan and cook under the preheated grill until bubbling and brown.

Divide the lentils between 4 individual plates, scatter over the remaining onion and top with the tomatoes. Carefully lift the cheeses from the grill pan and arrange on top of the lentils. Scatter over the pine kernels and the coriander and serve immediately.

Hot Chilli Pasta
30 minutes to the table

SERVES 4

ingredients

150 ml/5 fl oz dry white wine

1 tbsp sun-dried tomato paste

2 fresh red chillies

2 garlic cloves, finely chopped

350 g/12 oz dried tortiglioni

4 tbsp chopped fresh flat-leaf parsley

salt and pepper

fresh shavings of pecorino cheese,
   to garnish

SUGOCASA

5 tbsp extra-virgin olive oil

450 g/1 lb plum tomatoes, chopped

salt and pepper

method

To make the sugocasa, heat the oil in a frying pan over a high heat until almost smoking. Add the tomatoes and cook, stirring, for 2-3 minutes. Reduce the heat to low and cook for 20 minutes, or until very soft. Season to taste with salt and pepper, then pass through a food mill or press through a fine, non-metallic sieve into a clean saucepan.

Add the wine, tomato paste, chillies and garlic to the sugocasa and bring to the boil. Reduce the heat and simmer gently.

Meanwhile, bring a large saucepan of lightly salted water to the boil. Add the pasta, return to the boil and cook for 8-10 minutes, or according to the packet instructions, until tender but still firm to the bite.

Meanwhile, remove the chillies from the sugocasa and taste the sauce. If you prefer a hotter flavour, chop some or all of the chillies and return them to the saucepan. Check the seasoning at the same time, then stir in half the parsley.

Drain the pasta and tip into a warmed serving bowl. Add the sauce and toss to coat. Sprinkle with the remaining parsley, garnish with the shavings of pecorino cheese and serve immediately.

cook's tip

If time is short, use ready-made sugocasa, available from most supermarkets and sometimes labelled crushed tomatoes. Failing that, you could use passata, but the sauce will be thinner.

Aubergine and Bean Curry

20 minutes to the table

method

Heat the oil in a preheated wok or large frying pan over a high heat. Add the onion, garlic and chillies and stir-fry for 1-2 minutes. Add the curry paste and stir-fry for 1-2 minutes.

Add the aubergine and stir-fry for 3-4 minutes, or until beginning to soften. (You may need to add a little more oil as aubergine soaks it up quickly.) Add all the beans and stir-fry for 2 minutes.

Pour in the stock and add the creamed coconut, soy sauce, sugar and lime leaves. Bring slowly to the boil and cook, stirring, until the coconut has dissolved. Stir in the coriander and serve immediately, garnished with extra lime leaves, if you like.

SERVES 4

ingredients

about 2 tbsp vegetable or groundnut oil

1 onion, chopped

2 garlic cloves, crushed

2 fresh red chillies, deseeded and chopped

1 tbsp Thai red curry paste

1 large aubergine, cut into chunks

115 g/4 oz pea or small aubergines

115 g/4 oz shelled baby broad beans

115 g/4 oz fine French beans

300 ml/10 fl oz vegetable stock

55 g/2 oz creamed coconut, chopped

3 tbsp Thai soy sauce

1 tsp palm sugar or soft light brown sugar

3 kaffir lime leaves, roughly torn, plus extra whole leaves to garnish (optional)

4 tbsp chopped fresh coriander

Broccoli with Peanuts
20 minutes to the table

SERVES 4

ingredients

3 tbsp vegetable or groundnut oil

1 lemon grass stalk, outer leaves
   removed, roughly chopped

2 fresh red chillies, deseeded and
   chopped

2.5-cm/1-inch piece fresh root ginger,
   grated

3 kaffir lime leaves, roughly torn

3 tbsp Thai green curry paste

1 onion, chopped

1 red pepper, deseeded and chopped

350 g/12 oz broccoli, cut into florets

115 g/4 oz fine French beans

55 g/2 oz unsalted peanuts

method

Put 2 tablespoons of the oil, the lemon grass, chillies, ginger, lime leaves and curry paste into a food processor and process to a paste.

Heat the remaining oil in a preheated wok or large frying pan over a high heat. Add the spice paste, onion and red pepper and stir-fry for 2–3 minutes until beginning to soften.

Stir in the broccoli and beans. Reduce the heat to low, cover and cook, stirring occasionally, for 4–5 minutes until tender.

Meanwhile, dry-fry the peanuts in a heavy-based frying pan until lightly browned. Add to the broccoli mixture and toss together. Serve immediately.

Courgette and Cashew Nut Curry

15 minutes to the table

method

Heat the oil in a preheated wok or large frying pan over a high heat. Add the onions, garlic and chillies and stir-fry for 1–2 minutes until softened but not browned.

Add the courgettes and mushrooms and stir-fry for 2–3 minutes until tender.

Add the beansprouts, cashew nuts, chopped chives, soy sauce and fish sauce, if using, and stir-fry for 1–2 minutes.

Serve the curry immediately, garnished with whole chives.

cook's tip

Try to find small courgettes. If you have to use larger ones, you may need to cut the slices in half before cooking.

SERVES 4

ingredients

2 tbsp vegetable or groundnut oil

6 spring onions, chopped

2 garlic cloves, chopped

2 fresh green chillies, deseeded
  and chopped

450 g/1 lb courgettes,
  cut into thick slices

115 g/4 oz shiitake mushrooms, halved

55 g/2 oz fresh beansprouts

85 g/3 oz cashew nuts, dry-fried

few fresh Chinese chives, chopped,
  plus whole chives to garnish

4 tbsp Thai soy sauce

1 tsp Thai fish sauce (optional)

Spiced Pumpkin and Coconut

25 minutes to the table

method

If you are using a whole coconut, pierce with a skewer to punch a hole in the 'eye' of the coconut, then pour out and reserve the liquid from the inside.

Measure the coconut liquid and add water, if necessary, to make 250 ml/9 fl oz. Add the chilli, sugar, coriander, cumin, chilli powder and bay leaves to the coconut liquid and set aside.

Break the coconut in half against a hard, durable surface, then peel half the coconut and grate the flesh on the coarse side of a grater or process in a food processor.

Melt the ghee in a preheated kadhai, wok or large frying pan over a medium heat. Add the pumpkin and stir-fry for 1 minute. Add the grated coconut and stir-fry until the mixture is beginning to turn brown.

Stir in the coconut liquid. Increase the heat and continue to stir-fry until only about 4 tablespoons of liquid are left. Sprinkle with the garam masala and continue to stir-fry until all the liquid has evaporated. Serve immediately.

cook's tip

If you can't find a fresh coconut, use 125 g/4½ oz desiccated coconut and stir-fry the pumpkin and coconut in a mixture of 125 g/4½ oz creamed coconut dissolved in 250 ml/9 fl oz boiling water.

SERVES 4-6

ingredients

1 fresh coconut
1 fresh green chilli, deseeded
    and chopped
1½ tsp sugar
1 tsp ground coriander
¾ tsp ground cumin
¼ tsp chilli powder
2 bay leaves
25 g/1 oz ghee or 2 tbsp vegetable
    or groundnut oil
600 g/1 lb 5 oz pumpkin, peeled,
    deseeded and coarsely grated
1 tsp garam masala

Matar Paneer
30 minutes to the table

SERVES 4

ingredients

about 85 g/3 oz ghee or 6 tbsp
    vegetable or groundnut oil
350 g/12 oz paneer,
    cut into 1-cm/½-inch pieces
2 large garlic cloves, chopped
1-cm/½-inch piece fresh root ginger,
    finely chopped
1 large onion, finely sliced
1 tsp ground turmeric
1 tsp garam masala
¼–½ tsp chilli powder
350 g/12 oz frozen peas
1 fresh bay leaf
½ tsp salt
125 ml/4 fl oz water
chopped fresh coriander, to garnish

method

Heat the ghee in a large frying pan or flameproof casserole with a tight-fitting lid over a medium-high heat. Add as many paneer pieces as will fit in a single layer without overcrowding the pan and cook for 5 minutes until golden brown all over. Remove with a slotted spoon and drain on crumpled kitchen paper. Repeat, adding a little extra ghee, if necessary, until all the paneer is fried.

Reheat the pan with the ghee. Stir in the garlic, ginger and onion and cook, stirring frequently, for 5 minutes, or until the onion is softened but not browned.

Stir in the turmeric, garam masala and chilli powder and cook, stirring, for a further 2 minutes.

Add the peas, bay leaf and salt to taste to the frying pan and stir well. Pour in the water and bring to the boil. Reduce the heat to very low, then cover and simmer for 5 minutes, or until the peas are tender.

Gently return the paneer to the pan. Simmer, stirring gently, until the paneer is heated through. Taste and adjust the seasoning, if necessary. Sprinkle with coriander to garnish and serve immediately.

cook's tip

Paneer is an unsalted, mild Indian cheese, but is more like firm tofu in taste and texture. Available in blocks that can be cut into cubes and cooked without melting, it is an ideal vegetarian source of protein.

Chilli-yogurt Mushrooms
30 minutes to the table

method

Melt the ghee in a preheated kadhai, wok or large frying pan over a medium-high heat. Add the onions and cook, stirring frequently, for 5-8 minutes until golden. Stir in the garlic and cook, stirring, for a further 2 minutes.

Add the tomatoes with their juice and stir well, then add the turmeric, garam masala and chilli powder and cook, stirring, for 3 minutes.

Add the mushrooms, sugar and salt to taste and cook, stirring frequently, for 8 minutes, or until they have given off their liquid and are soft and tender.

Turn off the heat, then stir in the yogurt, a little at a time, beating vigorously to prevent it curdling. Taste and adjust the seasoning, if necessary. Sprinkle with coriander to garnish and serve immediately.

cook's tip

Adding the salt with the mushrooms draws out their moisture, giving extra flavour to the juices.

SERVES 4-6

ingredients

55 g/2 oz ghee or 4 tbsp vegetable or groundnut oil

2 large onions, chopped

4 large garlic cloves, crushed

400 g/14 oz canned chopped tomatoes in juice

1 tsp ground turmeric

1 tsp garam masala

½ tsp chilli powder

750 g/1 lb 10 oz chestnut mushrooms, thickly sliced

pinch of sugar

125 ml/4 fl oz natural yogurt

salt

chopped fresh coriander and coriander sprigs, to garnish

Mexican Tomato Salad
15 minutes to the table

Method

Put the tomatoes and onion into a large serving bowl and mix well. Stir in the beans.

Mix the chilli, coriander, oil, garlic and lime juice together in a jug and season to taste with salt and pepper.

Pour the dressing over the salad and toss thoroughly to coat. Serve immediately or cover and chill in the refrigerator until required.

variations

You could substitute 2 canned chipotle chillies, drained and rinsed, for the fresh chilli, and broad beans for the kidney beans, if you prefer.

cook's tip

You can make this salad in advance and store it in the refrigerator, but let it return to room temperature before serving.

SERVES 4

ingredients

600 g/1 lb 5 oz tomatoes, peeled, deseeded and roughly chopped

1 onion, thinly sliced and separated into rings

400 g/14 oz canned kidney beans, drained and rinsed

1 fresh green chilli, deseeded and thinly sliced

3 tbsp chopped fresh coriander

3 tbsp olive oil

1 garlic clove, finely chopped

4 tbsp lime juice

salt and pepper

Vegetarian Fajitas
25 minutes to the table

SERVES 6

ingredients

2 tbsp corn oil

2 onions, thinly sliced

2 garlic cloves, finely chopped

2 green peppers, deseeded and sliced

2 red peppers, deseeded and sliced

4 fresh green chillies, deseeded
    and sliced

2 tsp chopped fresh coriander

12 wheat tortillas

225 g/8 oz mushrooms, sliced

salt and pepper

method

Heat the oil in a heavy-based frying pan over a low heat. Add the onions and garlic and cook, stirring occasionally, for 5 minutes, or until the onions are softened. Stir in the green and red peppers, chillies and coriander and cook, stirring occasionally, for 10 minutes.

Meanwhile, dry-fry the tortillas, one at a time, for 30 seconds on each side in a separate frying pan. Alternatively, stack the tortillas and heat in a microwave oven according to the packet instructions.

Add the mushrooms to the vegetable mixture and cook over a medium heat, stirring constantly, for 3 minutes. Season to taste with salt and pepper. Divide the vegetables between the tortillas, roll up and serve immediately.

variation

If you don't like dishes too hot, use 2 fresh chillies instead of 4. The fajitas are good served with natural yogurt or soured cream.

cook's tip

Always wash your hands after handling chillies and avoid touching your lips or eyes. If you have sensitive skin, wear rubber gloves.

Index